BLOCK GRANT
1997-98

A BOSNIAN FAMILY

A BOSNIAN FAMILY

By Robin Landew Silverman

Heritage Middle School IMC
121 W. Butler Avenue
West St. Paul, MN 55118

Lerner Publications Company • Minneapolis

The interviews for this book were conducted in the summer and fall of 1994 and in 1995.

Copyright © 1997 by Lerner Publications Company

This book is available in two editions:
Library binding by Lerner Publications Company
Soft cover by First Avenue Editions
241 First Avenue North
Minneapolis, MN 55401
ISBN: 0–8225–3404–5 (lib. bdg.)
ISBN: 0–822–9754–3 (pbk.)

A pronunciation guide can be found on page 62.

LIBRARY OF CONGRESS CATALOGING-IN-PUBLICATION DATA

Silverman, Robin Landew
  A Bosnian family / by Robin Landew Silverman.
    cm. — (Journey between two worlds)
  Includes index.
  Summary: Describes the events that led to war in the former Yugoslavia and the efforts of one family to escape from Bosnia and make a new life in Grand Forks, North Dakota. Includes a Yugoslavian folktale.
  ISBN 0–8225–3404–5 (lib. bdg. : alk. paper)
  1. Bosnian American families—North Dakota—Grand Forks—Case studies—Juvenile literature. 2. Bosnian Americans—North Dakota—Grand Forks—Case studies—Juvenile literature. 3. Refugees, Political—North Dakota—Grand Forks—Case studies—Juvenile literature. 4. Refugees, Political—Bosnia—Case studies—Juvenile literature. 5. Grand Forks (N.D.)—Social life and customs—Juvenile literature. [1. Bosnian Americans. 2. Refugees.]
I. Title. II. Series
F644.G8S55   1996
304.8′78416—dc20   95–46971

Manufactured in the United States of America
1 2 3 4 5 6 – SP – 02 01 00 99 98 97

AUTHOR'S NOTE

This book would not have been possible without the warm, generous welcome, the constant, trusting friendship, and the stunning bravery of the Dusper family. Their hope in opening their home and their lives to thousands of readers was to help people understand the horrors of war and the need for lasting peace in our lifetime.

So, to the Duspers, I offer my most profound thanks. To my husband and collaborator, Stephen, I treasure your support and delight in yet another adventure taken together. Your photos bring out the beauty in every subject you approach. To my daughters, Amanda and Erica, thanks for all the days when you took care of yourselves so I could take care of this—and for your endless patience in reading the manuscript pages. And to my incredibly supportive parents, thanks for the typewriter, the notes, and the purple sweater. I love you all.

The parliament building (above) in downtown Sarajevo, the capital of Bosnia, burns after being hit with an artillery shell during the civil war. The conflict in Bosnia, an eastern region of the former Yugoslavia, began after the republic declared its independence in the spring of 1992. Hundreds of Bosnian families (facing page) who were forced to flee their homes because of the fighting seek refuge in a school gymnasium.

SERIES INTRODUCTION

 What they have left behind is sometimes a living nightmare of war and hunger that most Americans can hardly begin to imagine. As refugees set out to start a new life in another country, they are torn by many feelings. They may wish they didn't have to leave their homeland. They may fear giving up the only life they have ever known. Many may also feel excitement and hope as they struggle to build a better life in a new country.

People who move from one place to another are called migrants. Two types of migrants are immigrants and refugees. Immigrants choose to leave their homelands, usually to improve their standards of living. They may be leaving behind poverty, famine (hunger), or a failing economy. They may be pursuing a better job or reuniting with family members.

Refugees, on the other hand, often have no choice but to flee their homeland to protect their own personal safety. How could anyone be in so much danger?

The government of his or her country is either unable or unwilling to protect its citizens from persecution, or cruel treatment. In many cases, the government is actually the cause of the persecution. Government leaders or another group within the country may be persecuting anyone of a certain race, religion, or ethnic background. Or they may persecute those who belong to a particular social group or who hold political opinions that are not accepted by the government.

From the 1950s through the mid-1970s, the number of refugees worldwide held steady at between 1.5 and 2.5 million. The number began to rise sharply in 1976. By the mid-1990s, it approached 20 million. These figures do not include people who are fleeing disasters

Tiles top old buildings in the coastal town of Dubrovnik, Croatia. A civil war inflicted Bosnia's neighboring republic of Croatia after it declared independence from Yugoslavia in 1991. The conflict brought a sharp decline in tourism to Dubrovnik and other resort towns.

such as famine (estimated to be at least 10 million). Nor do they include those who are forced to leave their homes but stay within their own countries (about 27 million).

As this rise in refugees and other migrants continues, countries that have long welcomed newcomers are beginning to close their doors. Some U.S. citizens question whether the United States should accept refugees when it cannot even meet the needs of all its own people. On the other hand, experts point out that the number of refugees is small—less than 20 percent of all migrants worldwide—so refugees really don't have a very big impact on the nation. Still others suggest that the tide of refugees could be slowed through greater efforts to address the problems that force people to flee. There are no easy answers in this ongoing debate.

This book is one in a series called *Journey Between Two Worlds,* which looks at the lives of refugee families—their difficulties and triumphs. Each book describes the journey of a family from their homeland to the United States and how they adjust to a new life in America while still preserving traditions from their homeland. The series makes no attempt to join the debate about refugees. Instead, *Journey Between Two Worlds* hopes to give readers a better understanding of the daily struggles and joys of a refugee family.

A refugee and her son wait to hear if another country will allow them to enter its borders to escape the war in Bosnia.

The people of Yugoslavia came from many different ethnic and religious backgrounds. A mosque, or place of worship for Muslims (followers of Islam), overlooks the Neretva River in the mostly Muslim town of Mostar, Bosnia.

"Run, Zlatko! Run!"

Velma Dusper grabbed her six-year-old brother's hand as a bomb shrieked toward the town library. She had hoped to find a book to read, since the war had all but closed her school. Every day fewer and fewer children came to class. Velma didn't know if her classmates were dead, in hiding, or if they had escaped Bosnia for a new home in another country.

But right now, all Velma could think about was getting to her own home, the apartment she shared with her mother, Emina, her father, Nikica, her brother, Zlatko, and her cat, Kiki.

"Hurry!" Velma screamed.

As the two children raced home, their father was pacing at the window. Nikica looked relieved and happy to see Velma and Zlatko, but his voice was tense.

"Under the stairs! Now!"

The family took cover as more bombs fell. Every day the war that had started in the eastern republics of what was once the country of Yugoslavia crept closer to Velma's hometown of Bugojno. There was fighting in the surrounding mountains, and bombs could be heard in the distance. Sometimes they had landed close to town, but never *in* town, like on this spring day in 1994.

People in Bugojno also faced the danger of getting hit by snipers. These soldiers hid in alleys and on rooftops and shot anyone they saw. Simply walking down the street could be deadly.

A line of cars turned on their sides helps protect this group from sniper fire.

As Velma sat under the stairs, she wondered what her friends Maja and Irina were doing. Their family had left Bosnia two years before, hoping to start a new life in England. Velma had seen a picture of them which had been taken in London and sent to Maja and Irina's aunt. They looked happy and safe. As another bomb fell, Velma wished she were with them.

"I'm hungry," Zlatko said.

Nikica's thin face darkened. "We have some flour and water. That's all."

The family was almost starving. Before the war, the Duspers had lived a prosperous life. For the better part of two years, however, the family had eaten only small amounts of food. Bugojno's plentiful outdoor markets selling fresh produce were long gone. The fighting had destroyed most of the farms in the area. The farmers who were still growing crops didn't dare bring their produce to town, for fear someone would rob or shoot them.

Even if the markets were open, it wouldn't have mattered. No one in town had any money to buy anything, because it was impossible to get to work. Neither Nikica nor Emina had worked in almost three years. Snipers shot people who tried to get to their jobs. The men in Bosnia were forced to work for the army at no pay or else be killed. Nikica decided it was better to hide than to fight a senseless, cruel war.

Colorful outdoor markets, once common in Bosnian cities and towns, became a rare sight during the war.

Located in south central Europe, Bosnia was once part of Yugoslavia, a country of great natural beauty, many different peoples, and conflict. Towering mountains, swift rivers, soaring rock formations, fascinating underground caves, and a warm seacoast are all part of the region. Many residents have ancestors who came to Yugoslavia from nearby countries, including Albania, Turkey, Hungary, Austria, and Romania. Yugoslavia was once referred to as a place where citizens respected differences among people. But for most of the region's history that was not the case.

Differences in religion, language, politics, and even lifestyle have divided communities, causing fear and resentment. By 1990 these differences led to the end of Yugoslavia as the world knew it.

For half a century, Yugoslavia was a country that consisted of six republics. Beginning in 1991, four of them (Bosnia, Croatia, Macedonia, and Slovenia) declared independence. The remaining republics—Serbia and Montenegro—are still united. These two republics, as well as the provinces of Kosovo and Vojvodina, now make up the nation of Yugoslavia.

A castle rests above Lake Bled in Bled, Slovenia, near Austria.

 The former Yugoslavia has many neighbors. Albania, Bulgaria, and Greece lie to the southeast. Austria, Hungary, and Romania line the northern border, and Italy is a short distance to the southwest, across the Adriatic Sea. Because Yugoslavia was close to important sea and land routes, monarchs and sultans claimed the region for trade and military purposes. Throughout history Turks, Hungarians, Austrians, Macedonians, Serbs, Bulgarians, and Greeks have ruled the region.

WHAT IT MEANS TO BE MUSLIM

In most countries, people use the word "Muslim" to describe a member of a religious group that follows the teachings of Islam laid down by the prophet Muhammad in the A.D. 600s. People from many different ethnic backgrounds follow the Islamic faith. In the former Yugoslavia, however, Muslim also refers to an ethnic background. Many Muslims in the region are of Turkish descent—their ancestors came to the region from Turkey as many as 600 years ago, when the Turkish-run Ottoman Empire ruled the former Yugoslavia. Other Muslims were natives who converted from Christianity to Islam.

Muslims lived throughout the republics and provinces of the former Yugoslavia and made up the majority of the population in Bosnia. Many Serbs, as well as other groups in Yugoslavia, have resented the country's Muslim population. Muslims remind them of the more than 500 years the region spent under the leadership of the Ottoman Turks, who gave special benefits to the citizens of their empire who converted to Islam.

Alexander I

Tito

Over the years, leaders have tried to unite the peoples of this European region without success. In 1918 King Alexander I of Serbia was the first to take the independent republics and to create one country—Yugoslavia. In 1934 a Croat, unhappy with how much power Serbs had in Yugoslavia, murdered the king.

During World War II (1939–1945), hatred among ethnic groups in Yugoslavia grew worse. Josip Broz, known as Tito, organized a Yugoslavian army to resist Yugoslavia's king Peter as well as invasions by Germany. Not all Yugoslavians sided with Tito. By the end of the war, more than one million Yugoslavians had been killed, many by their own countrymen.

Tito's forces were victorious, and after World War II, Tito became the new leader of Yugoslavia. He set up a system of government similar to that used in the Communist-run Soviet Union. Tito opened new factories. He took cropland away from families and organized it into community farms known as collectives. The government discouraged people from practicing their religion. In addition Tito outlawed freedom of speech and strictly controlled all newspapers, radio and television stations, and other sources of information. A secret police jailed or killed anyone who spoke out against Tito. Under Tito, tension among ethnic groups in Yugoslavia was silenced. Most people did not risk expressing their hatreds for fear of arrest.

Factory jobs in Yugoslavia became more common in the 1970s and the 1980s.

Joseph Stalin, the leader of the Soviet Union at the time, tried to control Yugoslavia's growth in the 1950s. To ensure that Yugoslavia would not become dependent on help from the Soviet Union, Tito became friendly with non-Communist countries, including Great Britain and the United States. Through trade, loans, and aid, these countries helped Yugoslavia's economy and people prosper during the 1950s and 1960s.

By 1970 the Yugoslavian government had built many factories in towns along the Adriatic Sea. The people in these towns had good jobs and enough money to live well. But farmers were poor. Without modern equipment such as tractors and combines, the farmers could not grow many crops. What they could grow, they were required to sell to the government at low rates.

Farmers felt that the country's wealth should be shared. People in the richer, industrialized areas did not want to give away what they had earned. Tensions increased.

In 1990 President Slobodan Milošević declared the semi-independent province of Kosovo to be part of Serbia, claiming the region to be of historical importance to the Serbs. Muslim Turks defeated the Serbian Empire here in 1389. (Above) Muslims of mostly Albanian descent attend religious services in this seventeenth-century mosque located in Prizren, Kosovo.

When Tito died in 1980, Yugoslavia was a federation of six self-governing republics—Macedonia, Serbia, Montenegro, Bosnia-Herzegovina (often called simply Bosnia), Croatia, and Slovenia. The presidents of the republics agreed that each would govern the country for a one-year term. Before long, the strongest leaders began talking about making their republics independent nations. In addition Serbia, the largest and most powerful of the republics, had long felt that it should expand its borders to include the parts of Bosnia and Croatia that had large Serb populations.

The republics of Slovenia and Croatia soon declared their independence from Yugoslavia, against the wishes of Serbia. Few Serbs lived in Slovenia, but a large group of Serbs inhabited Croatia. They declared their own independence from Croatia, calling their new Serb state Krajina. A war began in Croatia, pitting Croats against Croatian Serbs. In 1991 Slobodan Milošević, the president of Serbia, invaded Croatia in support of Krajina. Within one year, the Serbian Nationalist troops occupied 30 percent of Croatia.

Milošević began a policy of ethnic cleansing. He ordered his army to murder or deport anyone who was not Serbian. Those who were not killed went into hiding or joined the resistance army. Many fled for their lives, leaving behind their jobs, schools, homes, families, friends, and possessions.

Slobodan Milošević

Alija Izetbegovic

Radovan Karadzic

Alija Izetbegovic, the president of Bosnia, is a Muslim who has wanted Bosnia to remain a state where people of all ethnic backgrounds are welcome. In the early 1990s, most Bosnians were Muslim, but Croats and Serbs made up some of the republic's population. In 1992 Bosnian Muslims voted to make Bosnia an independent nation. This angered Serbs who believed that Serb-populated areas should be governed by Serbians. Bosnian Serbs, led by Radovan Karadzic, wanted to unite parts of Bosnia with Serbia. A civil war began in Bosnia. Aided by Milošević, Bosnian Serbs

A Bosnian woman walks through the remains of her Catholic church, hit by artillery fire, in Sarajevo.

fought an army largely made up of Bosnian Muslims. Soon Bosnian Croats began fighting for their own state in Bosnia. The war in Bosnia pitted Serbs, Croats, and Muslims against each other.

Exaggerated reports of murder, rape, and torture between Serbs, Croats, and Muslims filled the news. Fear and hatred spread as each person began to feel they would be the next victim. Enemies burned each other's homes. Innocent civilians throughout Bosnia were tortured and executed, often by people who used to be their friends and neighbors. Serbian-run concentration camps housed starving prisoners of war. People from all ethnic groups suffered as the three armies fought.

By the end of 1992, about two million Bosnians from all three ethnic groups were homeless. Another 500,000 had left the republic as refugees. The United Nations, an international organization, sent in troops to halt the violence, but the efforts to make peace did not work.

The United Nations and countries around the world have worked cautiously to promote peace in Bosnia. Cease-fires have been established and then broken. Some people are hopeful that the parties will be able to settle their differences. Others are not so sure. No one knows if, when, or how the conflict will end.

Hoping for some relief from Serb attacks, Bosnian children welcome United Nations troops from Britain.

Velma heard her parents talking of escape. She wished they could go anyplace where their life could get back to normal. She wanted to go to school again. Because of the war, she was forced to leave school when she was 10 years old, in the fourth grade. It had been almost two years since she had been in a classroom. How would she ever become an archaeologist if she couldn't study?

Velma's family spent day after day under their staircase as bombs continued to drop. The family was barely surviving on flour, water, and an occasional potato. Her father would go out to try to get food from the Red Cross, an international organization that was sometimes able to bring supplies into the war zone. But since the bombing began, just going out onto the street was too dangerous.

Then one day, Velma heard the words she thought she would never hear.

A teenage Bosnian Muslim patrols the streets of the Duspers' hometown of Bugojno.

"We are leaving Bugojno," her father said. "You will take the bus to the refugee camp at Makarska with your mother and brother."

"But what about you?" Velma asked.

"I must walk over the mountains," Nikica said sadly. "I have paid a guide to help me. If I can reach Gornji Vakuf, where the Croats are in control, I should be able to board a bus to join you. But if I leave with you now, one of the armies will surely arrest me." Velma wrapped her arms around her father's tall, gaunt body. "Don't worry," he whispered in his low, soothing voice. "We will all be together again—and safe."

Velma wanted to believe him, but when she, Zlatko, and Emina boarded the bus the next morning, she had a sickening feeling that she might be waving good-bye to her father for the last time. Hiking in the mountains was dangerous in the early spring. The April air would be pleasant enough by day, but frigid at night, especially without shelter or extra gear. The melting snow would make each step uncertain. Even though her father was only 38 years old, Velma worried that he might get hurt or sick.

The bus ride to Makarska, located in Croatia on the Adriatic seacoast, took seven hours, more than twice as long as it did in peacetime. The driver had to detour around areas where there was fighting, and the few roads that were open were badly damaged from bombs and gunfire. The bus kept stopping in every small town to pick up more passengers. The people who boarded looked nervous and unhappy. Everybody was these days—including Velma.

Velma wondered if the people on the bus could tell where she and her family were headed. Emina had said that if anyone asked, the children should say they were going to visit their aunt in another city. To admit anything else might get them killed or thrown into a concentration camp.

Emina, Velma, and Zlatko took nothing with them— no clothes, no toys, not even a toothbrush. Before she

Bosnian refugees (above) *carry a few precious possessions as they cross the Sava River into Croatia, seeking a safe haven. Velma* (facing page, top left) *and her father, Nikica* (facing page, bottom), *recall his decision to escape Bosnia by climbing the mountains south of Bugojno. The former Yugoslavia is a mountainous country. The towering Alps* (facing page, top right) *cover much of the Adriatic coast, while smaller ranges blanket central Bosnia.*

About 10,000 Bosnian Muslims, forced to flee the Serb-held town of Srebrenica, board buses to various refugee camps.

left home, Emina packed one small cardboard box with the family's most precious possessions, mostly photographs and journals. She hid it in the house and hoped that a friend or family member who remained in Bugojno might send the box to them once the war was over.

The Duspers made it to the United Nations refugee camp without problems, but their worries were far from over. The place was teeming with thousands of Muslims, Croats, and others who had been made homeless by the war. What was once a beautiful resort city by the Adriatic Sea had become a city of last resort. Everywhere Velma turned, she saw wave after wave of somber faces.

When the Duspers were shown their living quarters, Velma understood why people in the camp were so sad. The camp assigned the family to one small room. Velma heard the drip of a leaky sink, but she didn't see a bath or a toilet. Those luxuries were down the hall in a bathroom shared by dozens of families. The Duspers didn't have a kitchen, either. Whatever food they got would be served in a communal dining area in another building.

"This food is ugly," Velma whispered to her mother as they ate later that day. "Canned meat and a tomato? Yuck."

"At least we are eating," Emina reminded her. "Your father may not be so lucky."

As night fell, Velma lay in bed and pulled her blanket up under her chin. She knew her father had nothing to protect him from the cold mountain air. She prayed that he would be safe. Then, for the first time in weeks, she fell asleep to the lull of the ocean rather than to the thunder of bombs.

Makarska is located in Dalmatia, a mountainous region on the Adriatic Sea.

 The next morning, Velma was ready to explore her temporary home. "Can Zlatko and I go play on the beach?" she asked her mother.

"Yes, but stay close, where I can see you from the window," Emina answered. "I want to stay here to wait for your father."

"But it will take at least three days for him to get here," Velma said.

"Even so, I will wait," her mother said firmly. "If there is any news, I want the camp officials to be able to find me."

So Velma and Zlatko went outside. The early April sun felt warm and good. Many children were playing on the beach, and before long, Velma and Zlatko were part of a happy group. The fact that the children were of many different ethnic backgrounds did not matter, as it had not when they lived in Bugojno. Without the influence of the war, children could be themselves.

Still, Velma worried about her father. He did not come that day or that night. If only they could call, if someone might have seen him. But there were no phones at the camp, no television newscasts, no way of knowing. Besides, for his journey to be successful, he would have to be as invisible as possible.

Velma tried to wait with her mother the next day, but being so close together in the tiny room made them all nervous. So Velma and Zlatko went back to the beach. The morning went by. Then the afternoon.

"Let's go back," Velma said to Zlatko as the sun was setting. "Maybe Dad is there."

Velma's brother, Zlatko, was six years old when the family fled Bosnia.

When they threw open the door, the biggest, strongest arms they knew swept them up in a warm embrace.

"Dad, you made it!" Velma cried as she hugged her father.

"Yes, I am here," Nikica whispered in a tired voice. "We walked all day and all night, without stopping. If we had stopped, we would have gotten frostbite. We had to bribe a guard in the mountains to let us pass, but he let us go. The next day, we made it to Gornji Vakuf, where there is no fighting. Then I was able to get on a bus to come here."

"You must be hungry," Emina said gently. "Come. We will go to the dining room and see if they will give you something to eat now."

 Ten days later, the Duspers applied to emigrate to the United States. Velma was excited. "English was my second language in school," she said confidently to her parents. "I will speak for us."

Passports (left and facing page, top) *were among the many papers that had to be processed before the family could leave Makarska.*

But Nikica and Emina thought of the difficulties that lay ahead. Velma knew only a little English, and they didn't know any. The parents realized they would have to learn the language and find jobs. But they also knew that they could not go back to their hometown. The children did not have a future in war-torn Bugojno.

"Will we go soon?" Velma asked.

"There are many papers that need to be processed, and we need a sponsor," Nikica said. "It will take some time. For now, let's go down to the beach. I want to go fishing."

Five and a half months later, on September 15, 1994, the Duspers left the refugee camp for Grand Forks, North Dakota. An organization called Lutheran Social Services of North Dakota agreed to sponsor the family. This meant the organization would help the Duspers start their new life in America.

The agency loaned the family money for airfare and gave them donated furniture and clothes. The agency arranged for the Duspers to receive some training in English. Other agencies in Grand Forks would pay for the Duspers' food and the electricity and heat in their apartment for the first three months. After that the family was expected to be working and supporting themselves. Within one year, the Duspers would also have to repay the cost of their plane tickets so other refugees could be rescued.

Lutheran Social Services of North Dakota, located in Grand Forks, arranged to get the Duspers out of their refugee camp and into the United States.

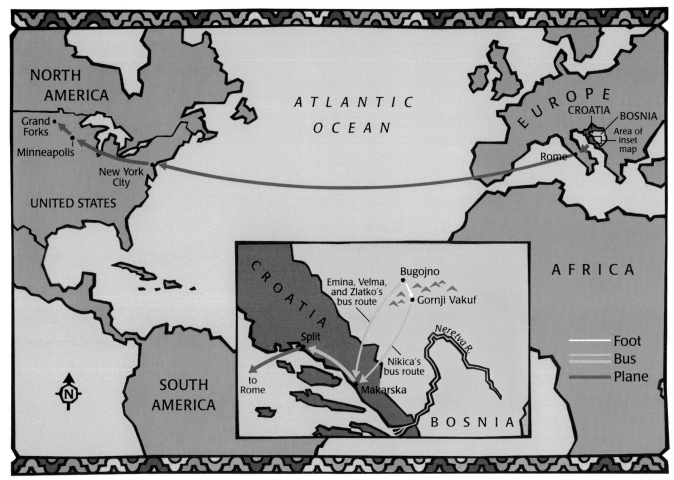

The Duspers' journey took them from Bugojno, Bosnia, to Makarska, Croatia. After spending about six months in a refugee camp, the family boarded a plane in Split, Croatia, and headed west, stopping briefly in Rome, Italy, in New York, New York, and in Minneapolis, Minnesota, before finally arriving in Grand Forks, North Dakota.

The journey from Bosnia to the United States took two days. It was the first time Velma or Zlatko had ever been in an airplane. Velma sat by the window. When the plane flew over the farms and small towns of the Midwest, Velma was amazed at the sight of miles of open land. All her life, she had lived in a crowded region.

With a bird's-eye view from the plane, Velma was surprised by the miles of open land she saw in the Midwest.

"Mom! Where are all the houses and people?" Velma asked. She certainly wouldn't feel cramped in this part of the United States.

The area looked peaceful and that was what mattered most of all. Velma imagined her family walking into a new apartment, *their* apartment. She knew that most Americans had plenty to eat, and she was happy that her family would not be hungry anymore. Her only concern was whether her new home would have mosquitoes. She *hated* mosquitoes.

 "Hello! Welcome to Grand Forks!"

A lanky young man with blonde hair and a soft smile approached Nikica and shook his hand.

"I'm Lorin, from Lutheran Social Services. I'll show you to your new home."

Many other people, including some Bosnians, had come to the airport to greet the Duspers. Nikica's

The Duspers arrived in Grand Forks in mid-September, as fall approached.

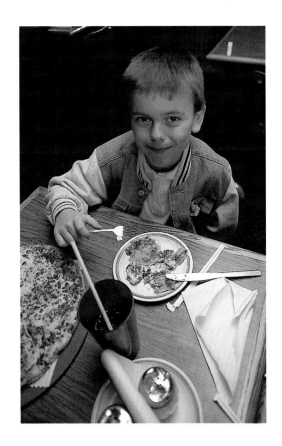

Zlatko tasted his first piece of pizza in a Grand Forks restaurant.

cousin Stravko and his wife, Mira, who had immigrated to Grand Forks the year before, were there too. Boris and Igor Princ, whose mother Kata arrived with the Duspers, also welcomed the family. Velma was glad to hear her own language as well as English.

The media came to the airport, too. The war in Bosnia was big news, and the arrival of Bosnian refugees in Grand Forks made a good story. The lights and cameras of the television and newspaper reporters flashed in Velma's face. Everyone was talking and hugging and nodding and smiling excitedly.

The Duspers quickly collected their few bags from the luggage carousel and stepped outside. The late summer's day was warm, full of sunshine and—mosquitoes! As Velma slapped one on her arm, she thought, "Oh, no! Not another nightmare!"

Although they were happy to be in Grand Forks, the Duspers were exhausted and hungry. So they stopped for their first meal in the United States—pizza. "I like it!" Velma told Lorin as she took another slice from the pan. "We don't have this in Bosnia."

The Duspers' apartment (top), *includes a kitchen* (bottom), *a luxury they'd been without since leaving Bugojno.*

The Duspers' apartment was a two-story walk-up just a few blocks from the school Velma and Zlatko would be attending. The dwelling was a lot like their apartment in Bugojno, only smaller. The family's American apartment had a kitchen, a living room with a stone fireplace, two bedrooms, and a bathroom. No more running down the hall to shower, as the family had done at the refugee camp! The place even had a tiny balcony that looked out over a quiet street. In Bugojno Velma had had her own bedroom, but here she would have to share with Zlatko. Velma didn't mind, though. She and Zlatko got along well.

People had donated furniture for them to use. It was old and worn—nothing like the beautiful modern things they had owned in Bosnia. But everything they needed was here in their cozy Grand Forks apartment, including dishes and linens. They were home.

"It is good. Perfect," her mother said.

Nikica nodded. Both he and Emina knew that the family had what they truly needed. For the first time in several years, they were living in a country without war.

They were in a peaceful place and truly safe.

Zlatko's teacher helps him learn to read in a relaxed setting (left). *Another student explains some school procedures to Velma* (below).

 The next day, Velma and Zlatko started school. Velma knew very little English, and Zlatko knew none. But that did not stop them from enjoying every minute of school. For the time being, everything was new and wonderful.

Velma's classmates had been told beforehand that a girl who had escaped the war in Bosnia would be joining them. Everybody, it seemed, wanted to help her with everything. One classmate showed her where to hang her coat. Others took turns explaining each worksheet and assignment. Velma was escorted through the lunch line in the cafeteria.

"Velma, this way!"

"Velma, like this!"

She was showered with attention—maybe a little too much. After all, she had not been in school for almost two years, and now she had a lot of work to do in a language she barely knew. She felt accepted, but frustrated, like a child who had to start learning from the beginning. Would she be able to be a top student again as she had been in Bosnia?

Zlatko had it easier in some ways, harder in others. Everyone in his first-grade class was just learning to read. And seven of his classmates also had come to Grand Forks from other countries, so he didn't feel different or self-conscious. But he'd never been in any kind of school before. It was hard for Zlatko to sit still all day.

Velma encourages Zlatko (top) *to read in English, a language completely foreign to him. Zlatko eats lunch* (left) *at the school cafeteria with his new friends.*

Numbers and counting came easily to Zlatko, and he mastered drawing on the new computers right away. But reading was hard. Really hard. So he and Velma started a school of their own at home. An American friend slowly read several stories in English onto a cassette tape. Every day Zlatko would follow along from the book. When Zlatko finished, Velma placed a star on a chart they posted on the closet door in their bedroom. Before long, the chart was full of stars, and Zlatko could read *Hop on Pop* and *The Cat in the Hat*, both by Dr. Seuss.

Nikica and Emina started school, too. They joined an English class for adults but found the language hard to learn. The teacher explained complicated grammar, when all they wanted to know were phrases that would help them shop, find work, and run their home.

"How do you say, 'Where is the grocery store?' or 'I need a job?' " Emina asked Nikica. She wished she had studied English when she was growing up in Bosnia.

One day Nikica's cousin took them to the supermarket for the first time. Emina was delighted to see so much food. She would be able to cook the family's favorite foods again, such as *pitta* (stuffed pastry), *sarma* (stuffed cabbage or grape leaves), and baklava (a honey and walnut dessert). She studied the fresh vegetables. "Just like the outdoor markets in Bugojno," she thought. There were some items, including broccoli,

When Emina first arrived in the United States, she could not read, write, or speak English. This complicated normally simple tasks such as grocery shopping.

that she had never seen before. Tomatoes and onions were favorites, and she imagined the Bosnian salad she would make by marinating them in vinegar and oil.

Emina bought beef and buttermilk, foods they all loved and missed. The variety of coffees thrilled her, since good strong coffee is a must in Bosnian homes. But when she looked in the bags of coffee beans, she was surprised to find that they came already roasted! She longed for the raw green coffee beans she had used at home in Bosnia and for the smell of roasting coffee beans in her own oven.

Emina filled her cart with everything she recognized, but then came trouble. She needed flour and sugar, but she could not read the English on the packages! She looked up as many words as she could in her dictionary before determining which sacks contained plain flour. Emina needed cornmeal, too, but couldn't find the word in her dictionary. She couldn't ask anyone because she didn't know how to ask in English. The purchase would have to wait.

Following a Bosnian tradition, Emina pours coffee for her guests in Grand Forks.

Emina skipped the aisles of frozen, canned, and prepared food. Most Bosnian women make their meals from scratch. Even though the family's new apartment had a microwave oven, Emina didn't care to use it. She believed that anything that wasn't homemade could not taste very good. In Bosnia she often spent two hours every day making dinner. And that's what she planned to do in the United States.

Emina bought far more than she would have if she still lived in Bosnia. There she went grocery shopping for the freshest food every day. But in America, she could only get to the grocery store once a week, when Nikica's cousin drove her there. The store wasn't on a bus route, and Nikica could not yet read enough English to take his driver's license test. Even if he could, the family didn't have a car. Life was better but not yet easy.

Nikica and Emina worried a lot about finding jobs. Nikica wanted to work in a dental lab, as he had in Bosnia. Emina had been a financial administrator in a Bosnian hospital. She didn't care where she worked in the United States, as long as her coworkers were friendly.

But finding work in the United States was difficult. Grand Forks had only two dental labs, and neither one

In prewar Bosnia, Emina shopped at a nearby market daily. In Grand Forks, where she depends on a car ride to the store, she buys a cartload of groceries weekly.

Soon after arriving in Grand Forks, Nikica found a job in a dental lab.

needed help. One lab, however, welcomed Nikica as an apprentice. As an apprentice, Nikica worked without pay so he could learn the English words for the skills he already possessed. He also hoped that in time a position would open up.

Eventually another lab offered Nikica a job making dentures (false teeth) for two days each week. Because he would not make enough money to support his family, Nikica also worked nights washing dishes at the pizzeria where the Duspers had eaten their first meal in the United States. "I will learn more English," he said. "I'll go back to school. Maybe learn computers. Then I'll get one good job." He sighed. "I must be patient."

Emina found a job at a pasta factory, separating broken pieces of lasagna from the good ones that would get boxed for sale. Her coworkers were friendly and glad to have her as a member of their team. The job paid well, too. But the work was tiring. Emina was on her feet from 8 to 12 hours, depending on how long her shift lasted. When she had to work afternoons or through the night, she did not see Velma and Zlatko at all for days.

Slowly but surely, the family's situation started to improve. With every paycheck, the Duspers would buy small items to make their apartment feel more like home—an ironing board, a pair of candlesticks, flowers. Eventually they had enough money for some lace curtains, and one of their American friends gave them a beautiful velvet sofa his family no longer needed. Emina bought a picture of an old man praying and put it and a Christmas tree ornament of the American flag on the walls of the living room. Zlatko and Velma's artwork from school decorated the children's bedroom wall. The family was starting to feel more at home in the apartment.

Emina works at a pasta factory (top). *Before long the Duspers could afford to buy small items* (right) *for their home.*

The next challenge was for Nikica to learn to drive a car. In Bosnia he either rode his motorcycle, walked, or took a bus. Cars in Bosnia were so expensive that it often took people years to save up for one. Nikica studied hard and easily passed the written test for a driver's license. The driving part was more difficult, especially on the icy winter roads of Grand Forks. But just five months after they arrived in the United States, Nikica passed the test and bought the family's first car—a 1985 Pontiac.

"Now we are not," Emina turned to Velma, *"Kako se kaze? . . . "* ("What is the word for? . . . "). She picked up the dictionary and pointed to "dependent."

"We don't have to get rides. If the person who drives us sleeps late or gets sick, we won't miss work."

"It is a good car," Nikica said proudly. "It starts the first time, and it has good acceleration. Now I go where I want."

Nikica sits atop his first car, a Pontiac.

 The warm, cozy smells from Emina's good cooking fill the apartment. She often makes "Bosnian Pot" (a stew of meat, potatoes, and vegetables) or homemade chicken soup with slender noodles. Sometimes she prepares baklava for dessert. Emina left all her cookbooks in Bosnia, but

In Grand Forks, Emina sometimes goes to great lengths to prepare traditional meals for her family. To make pitta (a stuffed pastry), Emina rolls homemade dough into a large, flat circle. She places small pieces of meat (or potatoes or spinach) on the paper-thin dough and folds it over before placing it in the oven.

47

Zlatko relaxes in the living room before supper.

another refugee gave Emina a bread recipe written in Serbo-Croatian. The Duspers often have a round, crusty loaf on the table at dinner.

Emina believes that the dining table should always be as beautiful and elegant as possible. She sets it for every meal with a small white linen tablecloth and linen napkins. Each piece of linen is pressed to perfection, and each fork, spoon, and knife is polished to a shiny glow. Their table always looks as if it belongs in a fine restaurant.

Emina prepares a feast for the family's first Christmas dinner in the United States. She will serve chicken noodle soup, sarma, and a marinated tomato salad. Then she'll surprise everyone with an American tradition—a roasted turkey!

"Christmas in America is good," Velma says as she puts the finishing touches on the family's tree. "In Bosnia we have trees like this. We would go to my grandmother's home in the country, and Dad would cut one for us.

"But I really like the lights," she adds as she and Zlatko hang a brightly colored string along their balcony. After the war began, lights were hard to come by in Bosnia. Even if you had them, you wouldn't put them on your house. Christmas lights would only help others identify your ethnic background, making you a possible target. "No one in Bosnia puts lights or

In Grand Forks, Velma and Emina are free to decorate the family's Christmas tree.

wreaths on their houses, because of the war. Here, it is very beautiful."

Before anyone takes a bite of the Christmas meal, Emina lights three red candles set in a wreath. Nikica closes his eyes and says a prayer in his native language. It is for thanks and peace.

 "Close your eyes, Ryan!"

Velma is a member of the makeup crew for the opera put on by her sixth-grade class. She is about to powder the face of one of the actors.

As a makeup artist, Velma participates in the production of an opera written and performed by her sixth-grade class.

Ryan squeezes his eyes tight as the softball-sized puff lands on his nose. A cloud of talc erupts all over his face and clothes. "Oh, no!" Velma laughs. "Well, you have much powder now!

"My class wrote this opera. We will perform it for the whole school soon," Velma explains. Velma puts the finishing touches on Ryan's face. She stands back to study her work, then shakes her head.

"No good. Too dark," she says critically, grabbing a towel and wiping off his face to start over. "He is supposed to be tan, from California. But this makeup is too dark. I'll try again."

Velma likes school. She says it is the best part of her day. Science and math are her toughest classes, even though she studied both subjects in Bosnia. English and social studies are easier for Velma. She has become a good reader and likes mysteries and horse stories best.

A tutor helps Velma with her schoolwork.

School in the United States is not like school in Bosnia. For one thing, the hours are longer. From first through fourth grades, children in Bosnia go to school for halfdays, either from 7:30 A.M. until noon or from 1:30 P.M. to 5:00 P.M. Only the older children go for full days. In Bosnia the children keep their books at home and the teacher tells them which ones to bring to school the next day. In the United States it is just the opposite. All books stay in school unless homework is assigned. Velma studies whatever she can in class.

"My best subjects are recess and gym," Velma says kiddingly. "Especially basketball."

"That's not completely true," her teacher, Mrs. Gregoire, says with a smile. "After only four months, she can read any book beautifully. She doesn't always understand every single word, but her comprehension gets better every day. And she's good in social studies and math."

"But science is still hard!" Velma added. "It's okay, though. In America I know I can become an archaeologist. That is what I want."

Velma has adjusted well to life in her adopted homeland. An able student, Velma is confident she will achieve her goals through the education she receives in the United States.

Meanwhile, Zlatko is mastering drawing on the computer in Mrs. Hamerlik's first-grade class.

"See?" he says proudly, pointing to a picture of a blue peak with a figure on it. "That's the mountain. And this guy is on the sled."

"Zlatko's good in math and art," his teacher says. "And his reading is really coming along. He's a favorite with all the kids, too. He keeps everyone laughing."

 With Emina switching between three different shifts and often working through the dinner hour, Nikica sometimes tries his hand in the kitchen.

"I make pizza," he says with a grin. "Not bad."

Emina has learned to use the microwave to save cooking time.

"At first I thought, 'I will never use that!' But it makes cooking fast," she admits. "The other day, I cooked dinner in little time."

Velma and Zlatko try many new things, too. Zlatko has learned to ice-skate and to sled. Velma already has these skills, but she still has to get used to playing outside in the bitter North Dakota temperatures.

"It was cold and snowy in Bugojno, but it is much harder to be outside here. The wind is so cold!" she says.

Playful and lighthearted, Zlatko has a reputation for keeping his schoolmates entertained.

BAŠ ČELIK

The former Yugoslavia claims many magical folk tales. "'Baš Čelik' is my favorite," Velma says. "I remember reading it when I was a little girl."

Once upon a time, there was a czar who had three sons and three daughters. The youngest son was the bravest and most loyal of all. When the czar was about to die, he called all three sons to him and said, "Dear sons, I want you to give your three sisters to the first suitors who propose to them, no matter who they may be. If you do not do this, my curse will follow you to your death."

And with that, he died. Soon after, three of the most horrible monsters the brothers had ever seen came to claim the sisters as brides. Remembering their father's words, the brothers were powerless to stop the monsters. And only the youngest brother was willing to bestow his blessing on them, calling after each monster: "Take her away and have a happy cheerful life with her!"

Day after day, the brothers worried about their sisters' fates. Finally, when they could stand it no more, they set out on a search to find them. They walked for three days and three nights, but found no sign of them. On the third night, the youngest brother kept watch as his elder brothers slept. Around midnight, a huge wave from the lake broke over the shore and put out his fire. Before the youngest brother could ignite it again, a three-headed dragon raced toward him! He battled it alone and killed it.

The brother set out to find fresh kindling for their fire. He saw a fire burning in the distance and headed for it, thinking he would ask for a few embers. The fire came from within a cave where nine cannibal giants were roasting a man on a spit. The youngest brother was terrified, but before he could run away, the giants spotted him and brought him into their camp. The giants talked of raiding a nearby village for food. The youngest brother was frightened but said nothing.

When they arrived at the village, one of the giants ripped up two trees by their roots, leaned one against the fortress wall surrounding the town and pushed the other toward the youngest brother, who was as clever as he was brave. "Oh, good giant, I cannot move it alone," he said. "Won't you help me?"

As each giant moved toward him, the youngest brother chopped off its head with his sword. Soon, all were dead.

The youngest brother wandered through the empty town, for everyone was hiding from the terrible giants. At last he saw a candle glowing in a tower, and climbed up its steps to find a princess hiding inside the highest room. She was the most beautiful girl the youngest son had ever seen. But as she slept, the brother saw a shadow moving along the wall toward her. It was a poisonous snake, ready to strike. He killed it with one blow of his sword. For this and for saving the village from the terrible giants. The king allowed the youngest brother to marry the beautiful princess. The two eldest brothers returned home, and the youngest brother lived happily for a while with his new wife.

One day, the king left for a hunt and gave the youngest brother nine keys. You may open the first eight doors and enjoy all my treasure," he said. "But do not open the ninth door, for there lies danger."

Indeed, the first eight rooms were overflowing with gold, jewels, and other riches. The youngest brother contented himself with them for a while, but soon, his curiosity got the better of him, and he opened the ninth door. There, he found the strangest, ugliest man he had ever seen shackled in irons to a chair. Just beyond the man's reach was a golden fountain and a cup.

"Please, kind sir, give me just one drink, and I will grant you an extra life," he begged. The youngest brother filled the cup. The man drank it in one gulp.

The strange man asked for water twice more, each time promising the youngest brother an extra life. The final time the man asked the brother to pour the water over his head. As the water ran down his body, the strange man's shackles crumbled. He sprouted two strong wings, and swooped down into the garden, stealing the princess and carrying her off into the night.

When the king arrived home, he was horrified. "You have freed Baš Čelik!" he cried. "No one can slay him. We are all doomed."

This story continues on page 56.

But the youngest brother wouldn't give up. He went in search of his bride, but instead, he found his three sisters. The eldest had married the King of Dragons. The middle was espoused to the King of Hawks. And the youngest was the wife of the King of Eagles. The three sisters were delighted to see their brother again. The three kings welcomed their brother-in-law who had treated them with dignity when they claimed their brides. The kings promised to help their brother-in-law in his fight against Baš Čelik, and all three offered him one feather from their wings.

After many more days and nights of searching, the youngest brother found his wife in the woods, tending Baš Čelik's fire. Three times, the youngest brother tried to rescue his wife. Three times. Baš Čelik granted the youngest brother an extra life, as he had promised. On the fourth attempt, Baš Čelik was about to strike when the youngest brother took out his flint and set the three feathers on the fire, signaling the three kings.

As the three kings arrived with their armies, the princess flattered Baš Čelik into sharing the secret of his strength. "There is a fox who lives on a high mountain far from this forest," Baš Čelik whispered. "There is a bird in its heart, and in that bird lies my strength."

Hearing this, the brother and the three kings set out to find the fox. But the fox was magical and could change shape at will. Just as the King of Eagles spotted him, the fox became a six-winged duck. When the King of Hawks was about to strike, the duck spread all its wings and soared into the air. But before the King of Dragons could set his wings on fire, the duck turned back into a fox. All three armies pursued the magical animal until it was surrounded and killed. They took out its heart and removed the fiendish bird, throwing it into the fire. As they did, Baš Čelik died.

The youngest brother returned to claim his wife, and they all lived in peace and happiness thereafter, since there were no more enemies to bother any of their kingdoms. And the blessings of their people followed the happy couple wherever they went.

This story is reprinted in an abridged version from Yugoslav Folk-Tales *by Nada Ćurčija-Prodanović (H.Z. Walck, 1966).*

Although the Duspers are happy in Grand Forks, they have not been able to forget those they left behind. Whenever Emina and Nikica cash their paychecks, they send money to their relatives in Bosnia. Nikica's mother sends cards and letters. Occasionally, the Duspers are able to get a phone call through to one of the war-stricken areas where family members remain.

But Velma would not be satisfied until she found her two best friends, Maja and Irina. She thought of them constantly and wondered if they knew she was alive. She had not seen or heard from them in two years. And because she was so far from her homeland, Velma was afraid they would never find her.

(Right) *Velma*, left, *is pictured in an old photograph with Irina*, center, *and Maja*, right, *her childhood friends in Bosnia.* (Below) *Velma made every effort to contact the two sisters in their new home in England.*

Velma tried calling telephone directory information in London, but there were no listings for her friends. She asked an American friend to contact the British Red Cross. The Red Cross required that Velma's parents fill out a trace document, a paper saying that the Duspers wanted to find Maja and Irina's family. Velma wouldn't, couldn't give up.

Nikica and Velma went to the American Red Cross office in Grand Forks to start a search. They took home a form that asked dozens of questions about the family. Velma spent an entire weekend trying to remember every detail. For inspiration Velma looked at a photograph of herself, Irina, and Maja smiling, arms around each other.

When Velma and her father returned the form, the man in the office said it would take six to eight weeks to do a computer search. Then it would be up to Maja and Irina's family to contact Velma. The Red Cross tries to make sure that everyone who is found wants to be found. Velma hoped and prayed that her friends would be so excited to see that she was searching for them that they would call instantly.

One night Velma had a dream that Maja was trying to tell Velma her London phone number. Velma saw one or two numbers, but then she woke up! She would just have to wait.

One night Velma dreamt that Maja was trying to show Velma how to reach her long-lost friends.

Velma has at least received her wish for her family to live a normal life again. The Duspers left Bosnia for safety and freedom. They paid dearly for it by leaving their family, friends, possessions, and jobs behind. No matter how much they love life in the United States, a piece of their hearts will always be in Bosnia.

"Maybe someday I will go back there," Velma says. "I would like to see Bosnia again. But there would have to be peace first for many years." She smiles. "You never know."

Emina holds up a photo album she hid in their Bosnian home before leaving for Makarska. After arriving safely in the United States, Emina contacted a relative to send the album and a few other family treasures to Grand Forks.

THREE WISHES

"I have three wishes," Velma said one day. "One: That there should be peace in the whole world. Two: That everybody should be happy. And three: That I find my best friends, Maja and Irina."

Velma's classmates wanted to add their messages to hers. Her friend Adam said, "We [Americans] have it a lot better than people in other countries."

Ryan, her partner in the class opera, added, "War isn't as cool as people think."

Her friend Michelle piped in: "Everyone should remember to be grateful for what they have."

Velma summed up their thoughts precisely. "Tell American schoolchildren," she said knowingly, "to enjoy the peace they have."

Note: Approximately 10 weeks after Velma began her search for Maja and Irina, both the Red Cross and a family friend from Croatia delivered the correct address and phone number. The girls talk and write frequently, and Velma hopes to someday visit her friends.

FURTHER READING

Burger, Leslie and Rahm, Debra L. *United Nations High Commissioner for Refugees: Making a Difference in Our World.* Minneapolis: Lerner Publications Company, 1996.

Children of Yugoslavia Staff. *I Dream of Peace.* New York: HarperCollins Children's Books, 1994.

Close Up Foundation. *War in Yugoslavia: The Return of Nationalism.* Arlington, Va.: Close Up Foundation, 1993.

Flint, David. Bosnia: *Can There Ever Be Peace?* Austin, Tex.: Raintree / Steck-Vaughn Publishers, 1995.

Ganeri, Anita. *I Remember Bosnia.* Austin, Tex.: Raintree / Steck-Vaughn Publishers, 1995.

Ricciuti, Edward R. *War in Yugoslavia: The Breakup of a Nation.* Brookfield, Conn.: Millbrook Press, 1993.

Rody, Martyn. *The Break Up of Yugoslavia.* Englewood Cliffs, N.J.: New Discovery Books, Silver Burdett Press, 1994.

PRONUNCIATION GUIDE

Adriatic (ay-dree-AT-ik)
Baš Čelik (BAHZ CHEHL-ihk)
Bosnia-Herzegovina (BAHZ-nee-uh-hehrt-seh-goh-VEE-nuh)
Bugojno (boo-GOHN-yoh)
Croatia (kroh-AY-shuh)
Dusper (DOOS-puhr)
Emina (eh-MEE-nah)
Gornji Vakuf (GOHR-nee VAH-kawf)
Irina (eer-EE-nah)
Izetbegovic, Alija (ihz-eht-BEH-goh-vich, ahl-EE-yah)
Karadzic, Radovan (KEHR-a-chich, RAH-doh-vahn)
Krajina (KRY-nah)
Maja (MY-uh)
Makarska (mah-KAHR-skah)
Milošević, Slobodan (mee-LOH-sheh-vihtch SLAW-baw-duhn)
Nikica (NIH-keet-zhah)
Serbia (SUHR-bee-uh)
Tito (TEE-toh)
Velma (VEHL-mah)
Vojvodina (VOY-vuh-dee-nuh)
Yugoslavia (yoo-goh-SLAH-vee-uh)
Zlatko (ZLAHT-koh)

INDEX

ABOUT THE AUTHOR

Robin Landew Silverman is a writer who specializes in real stories about how people make their lives better. Her work has appeared nationwide in newspapers and magazines, including the *Grand Forks Herald*, the *Philadelphia Inquirer, Inc., Catalist,* and *'Teen*. She is the creator of the "Love From Home" workshops and audiotapes, which help people discover the good in their personal stories. A native of Westfield, New Jersey, Ms. Silverman resides in Grand Forks, North Dakota, with her husband and two daughters.

PHOTO ACKNOWLEDGMENTS

Cover photographs by Reuters/Bettmann (left) and © Steve Silverman (right). All inside photos by © Steve Silverman except the following: Reuters/Corbis-Bettmann, p. 6; Reuters/Chris Helgren/Archive Photos, pp. 7, 12; © Don Eastman, pp. 8, 10, 13, 16, 20, 26 (right), 29; Reuters/Bettmann, pp. 9, 22; Laura Westlund, pp. 15, 34; © Giaconne/Zuma, p. 17; UPI/Corbis-Bettmann, p. 18 (top); Archive Photos, p. 18 (bottom); OPIC, p. 19; Reuters/Neal C. Lauron/Archive Photos, p. 21 (left); Reuters/Eric Miller/Archive Photos, p. 21 (center); © Russell Gordon/ZUMA, p. 21 (right); Archive Photos/Express Newspaper, p. 23; Reuters/Corinne Dufka/Archive Photos, p. 25; P. Kessler/UNHCR, p. 27; Reuters/Wade Goddard/Archive Photos, p. 28; South Dakota Dept. of Tourism, p. 35; Greater Grand Forks Convention and Visitors Bureau, p. 36; Velma Dusper, p. 58 (right); Robin Landew Silverman, p. 64; Lace and woodwork cut-ins by Nancy Smedstad. All artwork and maps by Laura Westlund.